TIDAL FLATS

By Melissa Cole

BLACKBIRCH®
PRESS

THOMSON
™
GALE

San Diego • Detroit • New York • San Francisco • Cleveland • New Haven, Conn. • Waterville, Maine • London • Munich

THOMSON

GALE

For more information, contact
The Gale Group, Inc.
27500 Drake Rd.
Farmington Hills, MI 48331-3535
Or you can visit our Internet site at http://www.gale.com

Photo Credits: Cover, all photos © Tom and Pat Leeson Wildlife Photography, except page 13 © CORBIS; pages 21, 23 illustrations by Chris Jouan Illustration

LIBRARY OF CONGRESS CATALOGING-IN-PUBLICATION DATA

Cole, Melissa S.
  Tidal flats / by Melissa S. Cole.
    p. cm. — (Wild America habitats)
  ISBN 1-56711-809-7 (hardback : alk. paper)
  1. Tidal flat ecology—Juvenile literature. [1. Tidal flats. 2. Tidal flat ecology. 3. Ecology.]
I. Title. II. Series: Wild America habitats series.

QH541.5.S35 C65 2003
551.45'7—dc21   2002015062

Printed in China
10 9 8 7 6 5 4 3 2 1

Contents

Introduction

There are many types of habitats found throughout North America. A habitat is a certain area where a specific community of plants and animals live. Tidal flats occur along North America's coast-lines, where the ocean meets the land. Tidal flats are wide expanses of sandy beaches. Along the high edges of many tidal flats, rolling hills called sand dunes are commonly found. Dunes form when strong coastal winds carry the sand inland.

Tidal flats are habitats that occur where ocean meets land.

4

Where Are Tidal Flats Found Today?

Tidal flats make up much of the Pacific coastline. They stretch from British Columbia, Canada, to Mexico's Baja Peninsula. The Gulf Coast and much of the Atlantic Coast also have tidal flat beaches backed by rolling dunes.

Dunes often appear along the high edges of tidal flats.

What Makes Tidal Flats Unique?

Tidal flats are a unique habitat because ocean tides cover them with seawater for part of each day. Tides are caused mainly by the pull of the moon on the ocean. As the moon orbits the earth, its gravity pulls on the ocean directly below. This causes a high tide that covers the tidal flats.

In most areas, the sea rises and falls two times a day. During high tides, waves push seaweed, rocks, and driftwood up on the beach. When the tide falls, waves only cover the lower part of the tidal flats. Because of changing tides, plants and animals only live beneath the sea for part of the day. When tides are low, water no longer covers tidal flats. Animals are then exposed to wind, rain, sun, and predators.

Left: During high tides, seaweed washes onto tidal flats.
Opposite: Tidal flats along the coasts of North America have a variety of climates.

Climate

Since tidal flats are found along North America from Canada through Mexico, they have varying climates. Tidal flats along the east coast of Florida and the Gulf of Mexico have warm, humid climates for most of the year. The West Coast, including Canada and the Pacific Northwest, is cool and foggy. Tidal flats along Southern California and the Baja Peninsula have a warm, windy climate.

Topography

Sand is created when waves pound rocks and shells into smaller and smaller bits over time. Beach sand can be quite different in both color and texture from one beach to another. This is because sand is made of different materials. For example, New England's beach sand is made of quartz, garnet, feldspar, and other hard rocks. Florida's beaches are made up of limestone, coral, and shells.

Scientists divide tidal flats into three main parts, or zones. The subtidal zone is the area closest to the ocean. It is covered by water, except during spring low tides. The area between the high and low tide marks is known as the intertidal zone. It is the widest of the three areas. It is covered and uncovered twice a day by incoming and outgoing tides. The splash zone is the area above the high tide mark. This strip of land only becomes wet when splashed by waves or during spring high tides. Some tidal flats have a fourth zone. This is the sand dune area above the splash zone. It is the zone farthest from the ocean.

Opposite: Sand is made of crushed rocks and shells. **Inset:** Starfish live in the intertidal zone.

9

Plants and Animals Adapt to Tidal Flat Life

Tidal flats are a challenging habitat in which to survive, since the sand is constantly moving. Sand is smashed and pulled by the waves and blown by the wind. Aside from a few rocks found on the beach, plants and animals have nothing but the shifting sand to cling to. Despite these difficulties, many living things adapt to make this habitat home.

Sand moves constantly in tidal flats.

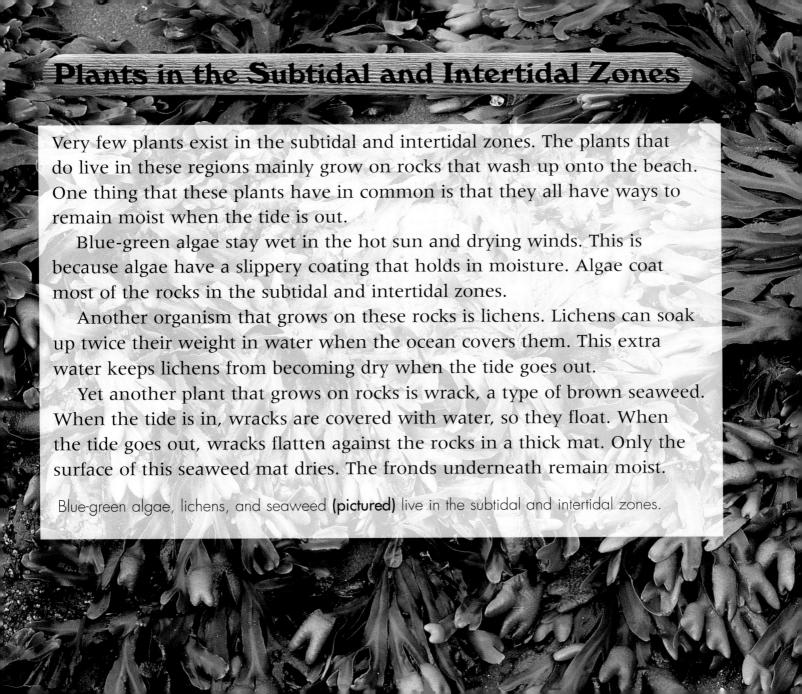

Plants in the Subtidal and Intertidal Zones

Very few plants exist in the subtidal and intertidal zones. The plants that do live in these regions mainly grow on rocks that wash up onto the beach. One thing that these plants have in common is that they all have ways to remain moist when the tide is out.

Blue-green algae stay wet in the hot sun and drying winds. This is because algae have a slippery coating that holds in moisture. Algae coat most of the rocks in the subtidal and intertidal zones.

Another organism that grows on these rocks is lichens. Lichens can soak up twice their weight in water when the ocean covers them. This extra water keeps lichens from becoming dry when the tide goes out.

Yet another plant that grows on rocks is wrack, a type of brown seaweed. When the tide is in, wracks are covered with water, so they float. When the tide goes out, wracks flatten against the rocks in a thick mat. Only the surface of this seaweed mat dries. The fronds underneath remain moist.

Blue-green algae, lichens, and seaweed (pictured) live in the subtidal and intertidal zones.

Plants in the Splash Zone and Sand Dune Area

Most tidal flat plants grow in the upper level of the splash zone and sand dune area. They are not usually affected by the changing tides. They are, however, constantly exposed to cold winds and salt spray, which dry them out. These plants have adapted a variety of ways to stay moist, though.

One type of plant that grows in the splash zone is called glasswort. Like a cactus, it has short, stubby stems and no leaves. To keep from drying out, it stores water in these stems during rains. Many other types of plants, such as American beach grass, sea oats, dusty miller, and beach morning glories grow on dry sand dunes.

Morning glory **(inset)** and sea oats **(opposite)** can survive on dry sand dunes.

It might appear that tidal flats do not have many creatures living on them. This is because most of the creatures live below the surface of the sand to keep from drying out. Tiny animals such as bacteria, worms, and shrimp live in the spaces between grains of sand. They feed on plankton that washes in from the sea.

Shelled animals such as clams dig down below the surface of the sand. Clams have two shells connected by a hinge. They have a soft body called a mantle inside their shells. A very strong muscle holds the two shells closed. A clam has a long tube, called a siphon, that it can push up through the sand.

A siphon pulls water inside the shell. The clam then filters out plankton to eat.

Clams filter their food from the ocean water.

Creatures in search of something solid usually attach to beach rocks. One of these animals is the limpet. Limpets stick to rocks with a round, muscular organ called a foot. Limpets use their rough tongues to scrape slippery bacteria off the rocks to eat.

Limpets eat bacteria they scrape from tidal flat rocks.

Another animal that lives on beach rocks is the barnacle. Barnacles build dome-shaped shells out of minerals they absorb from seawater. They feed by filtering tiny bits of food from the water with their feathery legs. When the tide goes out, barnacles close the opening in the middle of their shells to keep moisture in.

Mussels, which are bivalves like clams, often live alongside barnacles. These shelled animals begin life as tiny swimming larvae. The larvae settle on rocks, then send out small streams of fluid that harden to become tough, flexible strings. These strong threads attach the mussels to the rocks to keep them from being tumbled about in the surf.

Sand dollars are well adapted to living below the surface of the sand. Sand dollars have hundreds of feet, which are narrow tubes with suction cup ends. These tube feet help the sand dollar move across the sand.

Opposite: Goose barnacles live on rocks in tidal flats while sand dollars **(inset)** live beneath the sand.

Animals in the Splash Zone

Many of the tidal flat creatures that live in the splash zone are scavengers. Scavengers feed on seaweed, dead fish, and other animals that wash in with the tide. One of these animals is the ghost crab. Ghost crabs live in holes or burrows under the sand. During the day, their pale yellow color makes them blend in with the sand.

Beach hoppers, also known as sand fleas, feed on dead plants and animals that wash ashore. Sand fleas live on the surface of the sand. These shrimp-like creatures can grow to 1 inch (2.54 cm) long and hop more than a foot (30 cm) in the air.

Along all tidal flat zones, sea birds are the major predators. Seagulls scavenge food that washes ashore. They have also learned to drop clams and mussels onto rocky beaches and parking lots. This cracks open the shells so they can feed on the insides. Sandpipers, ruddy turnstones, sanderlings, and oyster-catchers feed on the tasty insides of shelled animals, as well as on other small animals.

Sanderlings **(below)** and oystercatchers **(inset)** eat shelled and other small animals.

Animals in the Sand Dune Area

A wide variety of creatures use sand dunes for shelter and protection. Many seabirds raise their young in the sand dune area. Insects hide in dune grass or in cool underground burrows. Frogs and toads breed in damp hollows between the dunes. Lizards and snakes bask in the hot sand on warm days. Among some dunes, predators such as foxes, raccoons, turkey vultures, and rats make their homes.

Royal terns live among the sand dunes of tidal flats.

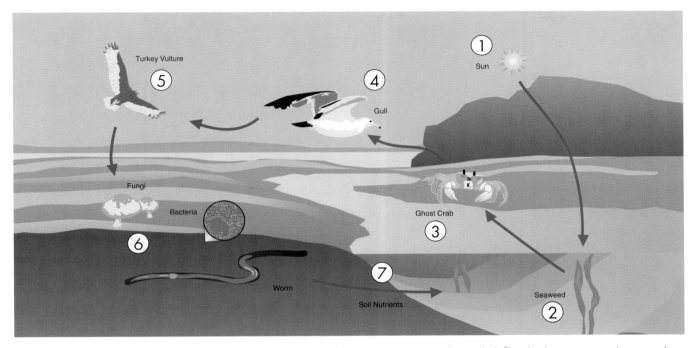

The food chain shows a step-by-step example of how energy in the tidal flat habitat is exchanged through food: **(1)** sunlight is used by **(2)** seaweed to make sugar, which is then stored in its fronds. When a **(3)** ghost crab eats the seaweed, some of the plant's energy becomes part of the crab. When a **(4)** seagull eats a ghost crab, the energy is passed from creature to creature. When the gull dies, scavengers such as **(5)** turkey vultures and beach hoppers feed on the waste. Decomposers such as **(6)** bacteria and worms break down the last bits and become part of the sand or mix with the seawater. Seaweed absorbs these **(7)** nutrients directly from water in addition to the energy that their fronds receive from the sun. Then the whole cycle begins again.

Humans and Tidal Flats

Half of North America's population lives along the coasts. When so many people live close to the shore, preserving the environment becomes a challenge. Development often changes the shape of beaches or causes them to erode away entirely.

Coastal pollution is another problem. Coastal pollution comes from sewage leaks, oil spills, and run-off. When it rains, water that contains pollutants washes into the ocean. These chemicals can soak into the sand and cause problems for many of the tidal flat animals.

Tidal flats are an often-overlooked habitat that needs protection. Humans can work together to keep the tidal flats and ocean waters a safe, clean habitat for the animals that live there.

Coastal pollution threatens the plants and animals that live on or near tidal flats.

A Tidal Flat's Food Web

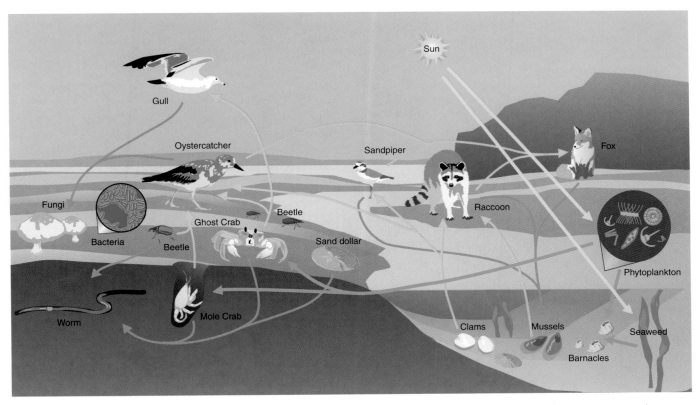

Food webs show how creatures in a habitat depend on one another to survive. The arrows in this drawing show the flow of energy from one creature to another. Yellow arrows: green plants that make food from air and sunlight; Green arrows: animals that eat the green plants; Orange arrows: predators; Red arrows: scavengers and decomposers. These reduce dead bodies to their basic chemicals, which return to the soil to be taken up by green plants, beginning the cycle all over again.

Glossary

Burrow A hole in the ground made by an animal for shelter

Dunes Hills of sand sculpted by the wind

Plankton Microscopic plants and animals that float through the ocean

Predators Animals such as seagulls, that hunt other animals for sfood

Prey An animal killed and eaten by another animal

For More Information

Books

Cumming, David. *Coasts*. Austin, TX: Raintree Steck-Vaughn, 1997.

Lawlor, Elizabeth P. *Discover Nature at the Seashore*. New York: Stackpole Books, 1992.

Pulley-Sayre, April. *Seashore*. New York: Twenty-first Century Books, 1996.

Websites

Surfrider Beach Cleanup site
http://www.surfrider.org

Index